My Science Library

Floating and Sinking

by Amy S. Hansen

Science Content Editor: Kristi Lew

Rourke
Educational Media

rourkeeducationalmedia.com

Science content editor: Kristi Lew
A former high school teacher with a background in biochemistry and more than 10 years of experience in cytogenetic laboratories, Kristi Lew specializes in taking complex scientific information and making it fun and interesting for scientists and non-scientists alike. She is the author of more than 20 science books for children and teachers.

www.rourkeeducationalmedia.com

Photo credits: Cover © Jules_Kitano, Michael C. Gray; Cover logo frog © Eric Pohl, test tube © Sergey Lazarev; Page 4 © Russlann; Page 5 © Daniel Gangur; Page 7 © Fotocrisis; Page 9 © Blue Door Publishing; Page 11 © Sascha Burkard; Pages 13 © Blue Door Publishing; Page 14 © Olinchuk; Page 15 © Sandra van der Steen; Page 17 © Lane V. Erickson; Page 19 © Kris Holland; Page 21 © ilFede

Editor: Kelli Hicks

Cover and page design by Nicola Stratford, bdpublishing.com

Library of Congress Cataloging-in-Publication Data

Hansen, Amy.
 Floating and sinking / Amy S. Hansen.
   p. cm. -- (My science library)
 Includes bibliographical references and index.
 ISBN 978-1-61741-738-2 (Hard cover) (alk. paper)
 ISBN 978-1-61741-940-9 (Soft cover)
 1. Floating bodies--Juvenile literature. 2. Buoyant ascent (Hydrodynamics)--Juvenile literature. 3. Archimedes' principle--Juvenile literature. I. Title.
 QC147.5.H36 2012
 532'.25--dc22
                                      2011003869

Printed in China, FOFO I - Production Company
  Shenzhen, Guangdong Province

rourkeeducationalmedia.com

customerservice@rourkeeducationalmedia.com • PO Box 643328 Vero Beach, Florida 32964

Table of Contents

What Floats? What Sinks?

Drop a dry **cork** in the water. What happens? It **floats**.

Now drop a penny. It **sinks.** What makes one of them float and one of them sink?

Take a close look at the cork. Can you see tiny holes? Those holes trap air. Air is lighter than water.

What Is Density?

Tiny **air pockets** are one of the things that makes the cork have less **density** than water. Anything that has less density than water will float.

That means a cup full of corks weighs less than a cup full of water.

9

Now look at the penny. The penny is made of **metal**. Metal does not have the same little holes.

Most metal has greater density than water. Anything that has greater density than water will sink.

A cup full of pennies weighs more than a cup full of water because of density.

Does It Float?

Test some other things. Will a carrot float or sink?

How about marshmallows?

If you guessed that a carrot would sink and marshmallows would float, you're correct. How did you know?

Why Do Boats Float?

Other things float. Boats float. Some boats are made of metal. The metal penny sank. Why do boats float?

The canoe skims the top of the water. What would make it sink lower?

Boats float because of their **shape.** Boat builders bend the metal to make a big air pocket. The air pocket lets the boat float.

air pocket

A canoe has one big air pocket instead of many tiny air pockets like corks or marshmallows.

Big ships float too. A ship's air pockets are big enough to float the ship and the heavy cargo it carries.

SHOW What You Know

1. A grape has more density than water. Does that mean it will sink or float?

2. Can you think of something that will float in water?

3   Why does a metal boat float?

Glossary

air pockets (AIR PAH-kits): enclosures that hold air in and are used for flotation

cork (KORK): a stopper used at the end of a bottle, usually made from the soft bark of a tree

density (DEN-si-tee): the amount of mass something has compared to its volume or size

floats (FLOHTS): rests on the top of a liquid or hovers in the air

metal (MET-uhl): a material such as iron, copper, gold, or silver that is usually hard and shiny when it is polished

shape (SHAYP): the form of an object

sinks (SINGKS): falls below the surface of a liquid

Index

Websites

www.kids-science-experiments.com/cat_floating.html

www.exploratorium.edu/snacks/descartes_diver/

www.tryscience.org/experiments/experiments_begin.
   html?buildaraft

www.tryscience.org/experiments/experiments_begin.
   html?oilslick

About the Author

Amy S. Hansen is a science writer who likes to practice her floating and sinking skills by swimming almost every day in the summer. She lives in the Washington, D.C. area with her husband, two sons, and two cats.